WAR HEROES

Written by Susan Brocker

They shall grow not old, as we that are left grow old

Age shall not weary them, nor the years condemn.

Laurence Binyon, "For the Fallen"

CONTENTS

Introduction

Many years ago, a young man saw two armies come face to face in a terrible battle. More than 40,000 men were killed, or left lying in agony on the battlefield. Nearby villagers were too scared to help the wounded, but this young man tried. He gathered up other brave people, and they did what they could. Still, many died. That greatly affected the young man, whose name was Henry Dunant. And so, in 1863, Dunant founded the International Red Cross, with the aim of helping wounded soldiers in times of war, whatever side they were on.

Above: *A helicopter waits for US wounded in Vietnam, 1969.*
Left: *Princess Diana was a volunteer for the British Red Cross campaign against landmines.*

Red Cross doctors in Afghanistan

Today there are other organizations, in addition to the Red Cross and agencies of the United Nations, that help people in war zones. Médecins Sans Frontières (Doctors Without Borders) provides emergency medical aid. War Child, formed in 1993, brings food, clothing, shelter, and medical aid to children in war-torn countries.

The heroes of war are ordinary men and women who have acted in an extraordinary way. Some, like Henry Dunant, helped the sick and wounded. Some performed heroically in battle. Others, such as the Colditz Castle escapers described on pages 26–45, showed remarkable qualities of invention and endurance. Most are unknown and their stories will never be told. Here are just a few stories that *have* been told, about courageous people who served in World War I (1914–18) and World War II (1939–45).

Henry Dunant

John McCrae

War Poet and Doctor

It was April, 1915. Some of the heaviest fighting of World War I was taking place in Belgium, in an area called Flanders. The once green fields were a sea of mud. Every blade of grass and every tree had been destroyed by mortar and shelling.

The soldiers fought from deep, muddy trenches dug in the ground. Among them crawled John McCrae, a Canadian doctor, on his way to treat the injured soldiers. One young soldier lay face down in the mud. John McCrae gently turned him over and looked into the lifeless eyes of a close friend.

John McCrae buried his friend alongside all the other soldiers in a shallow grave marked with a simple wooden cross. In the muddy ground between the crosses, beautiful wild red poppies were beginning to bloom. The flowering poppies brought colour, life, and hope to the sad fields. Moved by the sight, John McCrae took his pen and wrote:

In Flanders fields the poppies blow
Between the crosses, row on row
That mark our place; and in the sky
The larks, still bravely singing, fly
Scarce heard amid the guns below.

We are the Dead. Short days ago
We lived, felt dawn, saw sunset glow,
Loved and were loved, and now we lie,
In Flanders fields.

Soon after he wrote that poem, John McCrae was moved from the battlefields of the front to a field hospital in France. He was made Chief of Medical Services. The wounded were brought to him from some of the worst battles fought in World War I: the Somme, Vimy Ridge, Arras, and Passchendaele.

John McCrae worked day and night at the makeshift hospital, treating the injured soldiers. Yet, no matter how long or how hard he worked, he never felt as if he was doing enough. He wouldn't sleep in the officers' huts. Instead, he insisted on living in a tent through the freezing winter, like the young men at the front. When this made him sick, he had to be ordered back into the warm huts.

On January 28, 1918, John McCrae died of pneumonia. He was buried with full military honours in a cemetery near the fields of Flanders. His much-loved horse, Bonfire, led the procession.

John McCrae with his dog Bonneau, 1916

John McCrae wanted the world to remember all the soldiers who lost their lives during the war. His poem gave those young men a voice. Soon after it was published, it became the most popular poem of World War I. The poppy was adopted as the Flower of Remembrance for the war dead of Great Britain, France, the United States, and **Commonwealth** countries such as Canada, Australia, and New Zealand. People still wear the poppy to honour those who have died in war. It has become a symbol of hope – this small red flower that could even bloom in the midst of war.

Edith Cavell

Nurse and Rescuer

On a cold, wet night in November, 1914, two wounded British soldiers disguised in civilian clothes limped into a hospital in German-occupied Belgium. "Please, will you help us get back to England?" they begged the English nurse who was matron there. Nurse Cavell didn't hesitate, even though she knew she risked being shot for helping British soldiers to escape. She treated the soldiers, then smuggled them out of Belgium with the help of guides. The two soldiers were the first of many who would be hidden and cared for by Edith Cavell over the next year.

Since childhood, Edith Cavell had taken care of other people. In the village in England where she grew up, she ran errands and cooked meals for the sick and elderly. After training as a nurse, she went to Belgium to head a nursing school. She refused to flee from the invading German army when World War I broke out in 1914. She had a hospital to run.

As the German army marched into Belgium, **Allied** soldiers cut off from their units were left stranded behind enemy lines. They had two choices: to surrender as **prisoners of war (POWs)**, or to try to escape undercover from Belgium. But, if they disguised themselves as civilians, they could be shot as spies. If anyone helped them, they could be shot, too. Whatever the danger, Edith Cavell turned away no one who needed help.

Soon, many fugitive soldiers were coming to Nurse Cavell asking for help. She hid them in the hospital and cared for them until they were well and it was safe to escape. Then, she gave them money, identification papers, and guides to lead them along an escape route. The escape route was carefully planned by Edith Cavell and members of the Belgian **Resistance**.

Once, she had as many as eighteen soldiers hidden in her hospital. She helped not only British, but French and Belgian soldiers as well. She looked after them, tended to their wounds at all hours of the night, and ran the hospital. Only a few of her staff knew of her work, because she didn't want to put them at risk. By 1915, she had helped more than two hundred soldiers to escape.

One day, a man came to the hospital asking Nurse Cavell for help to escape. She hid him and cared for him. After he left, some of her friends in the Resistance were arrested. The man had been a spy. Edith Cavell knew it wouldn't be long before she was arrested, too. But she wouldn't give up her work. She continued helping soldiers, waiting for the dreaded knock on the door.

On August 5, 1915, the German secret police arrested Edith Cavell. She was sentenced to death by a military court and shot at dawn on October 12, 1915. Soon after her death, a statue was erected in Saint Martin's Place, London, in honour of her bravery. On the statue are her last words: "Patriotism is not enough," she said. "I must have no hatred or bitterness for anyone."

The memorial statue to Edith Cavell

Douglas Bader

Flying Ace

It was 1940 and the Battle of Britain was raging in the skies over England. The Royal Air Force (RAF) was struggling to defend Britain from German air attack. Waves of enemy planes were swooping across the country, dropping bombs on the ports and cities.

Scanning the skies for enemy bombers, Douglas Bader saw a bright glint of metal below. He flew his fighter plane higher and higher into the sky. Then he dived down, straight for a gaggle of German bombers headed for London, blasting them with machine-gun fire.

Only nine years before, this same pilot had been told he would never fly again. Douglas Bader had been stunt flying when the wing tip of his plane caught the ground. The plane cartwheeled and crashed. To save his life, the doctors had to amputate both his legs. The RAF said it was the end of his flying career.

But Douglas Bader did not give up. Slowly, painfully, he taught himself to walk on artificial legs. Once he could walk, he was back in a plane. Soon, he was stunt flying again, but the RAF wouldn't allow him to return to service.

In 1939, World War II began. The RAF was so short of trained pilots they had to let Douglas Bader fly again. He was given command of a fighter squadron that had lost many pilots. Morale among the men was low and, when they heard that their new leader was a man with no legs, it dropped further. But Douglas Bader's skill and courage gave them hope. Within a few weeks, he was leading a first-class flying team.

As squadron leader, Douglas Bader worked out clever fighting tactics. He taught his squadron to fly high into the sun to wait for German bombers. The blinding sunlight made them invisible to the enemy below.

In August, 1941, Douglas Bader had just shot down two German fighters over France when something hit his plane. The blow ripped the plane apart. As it plummeted towards the ground, he tried to climb out of the cockpit. One of his artificial legs was trapped! As the

wind roared in his ears, he struggled, until at last the leg broke and he could parachute free. The ground rushed up to meet him.

When he came to, German soldiers were bending over him. The Germans knew all about the famous fighter ace with no legs. He was well treated in a prison hospital. They even broadcast a message to England, asking that his spare leg be airlifted to him. But, as soon as he was back on two feet, he tied his bedsheets together, lowered himself from a window, and escaped.

He was recaptured and sent to a prison camp. Again and again, he tried to escape, only to be recaptured. The Germans didn't know what to do with this determined man. Finally, they locked him up in Colditz Castle, where the most difficult prisoners of war were kept. By then, his legs were damaged, and he stayed in Colditz until he was freed at the end of the war.

Douglas Bader believed that people could achieve anything if they had the will and the courage. For many years after the war, he travelled to hospitals around the world, bringing hope to children who had lost their limbs by showing them how well he managed on his own artificial legs. In 1976, he was knighted for his work.

Sir Douglas Bader and his wife at Buckingham Palace to receive his knighthood in 1976

Odette Churchill

Secret Agent

1943. Beside a disused airfield, a young woman huddled in the cold night. She could hear the distant drone of a plane and flashed her torch. The French Resistance desperately needed guns to fight the Germans, and it was her job to guide the plane to its secret landing place and unload the guns. Suddenly, the still of the night was shattered with the sound of yelling and dogs barking. German soldiers! She ran for the forest, the dogs snapping and growling at her heels. She plunged into an icy river and held her breath. The dogs ran past.

Odette Churchill escaped capture that night, but she knew her cover had been blown. It could only be a matter of time before the *Gestapo*, the German secret police, started rounding up the agent and members of her network.

Odette Churchill was an unlikely secret agent. Before World War II, she was a housewife living in England with her husband and daughters. But, when war broke out and her home country of France was invaded by Germany, she was recruited by the British Special Operations Executive (SOE). The SOE

World War II propaganda poster

trained men and women to work in Europe. Agents were dropped behind enemy lines to hinder the Germans and help local Resistance groups. The SOE needed ordinary French-speakers, like Odette Churchill, who could pass unnoticed in German-occupied France.

At first she did not want to join the SOE. She didn't want to leave her children. She knew that the job was dangerous, and that captured secret agents were almost always executed. But she also knew that many French people were suffering. So, as instructed, Odette Churchill told her family that she was training to be a nurse in the army, and went off to become a secret agent.

At a secret house in England, Odette Churchill was taught self-defence, **Morse code**, map reading, and tracking. She learned how to parachute from a plane, how to fire a gun, and how to destroy bridges, railways, and roads, using dynamite and plastic explosives. Most important, she learned how to pretend to be another person.

In November, 1942, Odette Churchill landed secretly in France to begin work with a network of secret agents under the code name "Lise". Her old self no longer existed. Even the English fillings in her teeth were taken out and replaced with French ones. She acted as a courier, travelling around France picking up stolen maps and documents to smuggle back to Britain. She found safe houses for agents and escaping Allied prisoners, and places for planes to land and drop off weapons.

After the night of her lucky escape, Odette Churchill guessed that her network had been infiltrated. Sure enough, on April 16, 1943, she and another agent were seized by the Gestapo. Odette Churchill was taken to Fresne prison in Paris and interrogated. The Gestapo wanted to know the names and codes of other agents, but, although she was tortured, she would not talk. In the end, she was sent to a **concentration camp** to die.

Odette Churchill did not die, however. Her brave spirit kept her alive. At the end of the war, she was awarded the George Cross, given only for acts of the greatest heroism and courage.

After receiving her award, Odette Churchill poses outside Buckingham Palace with her three daughters and her husband, Captain Peter Churchill.

Benjamin O. Davis Jr.

Red-Tailed Angel

On a bleak day in August, 1944,
a crippled American bomber was
rumbling across enemy skies when
a German Messerschmitt screamed
down on it. The bomber was too
battered for its pilot to take evasive
action. He felt like a sitting duck.
Then he saw a flash of red. A Mustang fighter with
a bright red tail dived out of nowhere to greet
the German Messerschmitt with a hail of gunfire.
The Tuskegee Airmen had arrived!

The Tuskegee Airmen were the first unit of
African-American fighter pilots. They fought in
World War II under the command of Colonel Benjamin
O. Davis Jr. One of the main missions of fighter pilots
was to escort bombers on their bombing raids over
Europe, providing them with protection from German
fighter planes. Although the US bombers were armed,
the lumbering machines were no match for the swift
and deadly Messerschmitts.

The Tuskegee Airmen earned a reputation as brave and loyal defenders. They stuck close to the bombers through the roughest spots over the target, where the danger of attack was greatest. They covered the planes as they flew through the **flak** and enemy fighters, and they escorted crippled bombers back home to base.

Soon American bomber crews were requesting that the Tuskegee Airmen escort them, rather than other fighter units. They called the Tuskegee Airmen the "Red-Tailed Angels", because of the brightly painted red tails on their fighter planes and the angel-like protection they provided. They were called the "Schwarze Vogelmenschen" (Black Birdmen) by the Germans, who feared and respected them.

Colonel Davis at the Tuskegees' Italian airbase, 1945

On one of his greatest missions, in March, 1945, Colonel Davis led his Tuskegee fighters on a bomber escort all the way to Berlin. This was a round-trip of over 2,500 kilometres to and from their base in Italy. Low on fuel and ammunition, the Tuskegee Airmen fought off wave after wave of German fighters. They even shot down three of the Germans' new ME-262s, the world's first operational jet fighters. No bombers were lost.

By the end of the war, the Tuskegee Airmen had been awarded 150 Distinguished Flying Crosses, many more Air Medals and Clusters, Legions of Merit, the Red Star of Yugoslavia, and the Presidential Unit Citation. Most important, they had flown 200 bomber escort missions against some of the most heavily defended targets in Germany without losing a bomber to enemy fighters.

Benjamin O. Davis Jr. retired from the air force in 1970 as a three-star general. In December, 1998, he received an honorary fourth star from US President Clinton, who described him as "a hero in war, a leader in peace, and a pioneer for freedom".

Left: General Earle E. Partridge presents the stars of a brigadier general to Benjamin O. Davis Jr. (left) in Japan, 1954. General Davis was the first African-American officer in the United States Air Force to attain that rank.

Escape from Colditz

Dark and foreboding, Colditz Castle towers above the town of Colditz, midway between the cities of Leipzig and Dresden in what was East Germany. The castle was once the most

Colditz Castle

famous of all the German World War II prisoner of war camps. Its grey granite walls and tall towers were the setting for legendary escape attempts. But how did anyone ever manage to scale those walls or climb those towers?

Some of the first British arrivals in Colditz. Pat Reid (far left) led the escape attempt described on pages 30–31.

Major William Faithfull Anderson was a British prisoner in Colditz from July, 1941, until the camp was liberated in April, 1945. His paintings of life in Colditz can be seen on pages 32, 39, and 42, and on the web site www.colditz-4c.com.

Built in 1014 as a hunting lodge for royalty, Colditz Castle became a prisoner of war camp in 1939, when World War II began with the German invasion of Poland.

By the end of 1940, the Germans had decided that Colditz Castle should become a *sonderlager* – a special high-security jail for prisoners of war who kept escaping from other camps. British, Dutch, and French officers arrived to join the Poles and Belgians already there. Perhaps it wasn't quite the neat solution it seemed, however – the Germans had brought together in one place the most determined and clever of all the POWs.

Colditz is built on a cliff, surrounded by high walls at least 2 metres thick, from which the ground falls away steeply in terraces. The Germans considered it escape-proof, but British prisoners had been in the castle for less than two months when they began to put that boast to the test.

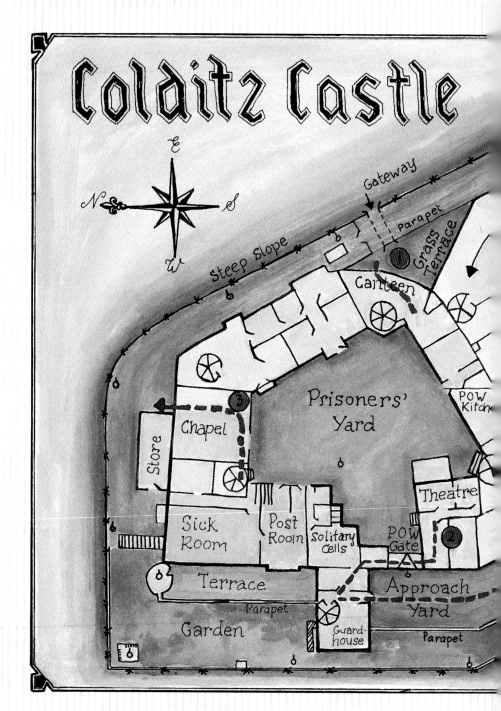

Colditz Castle

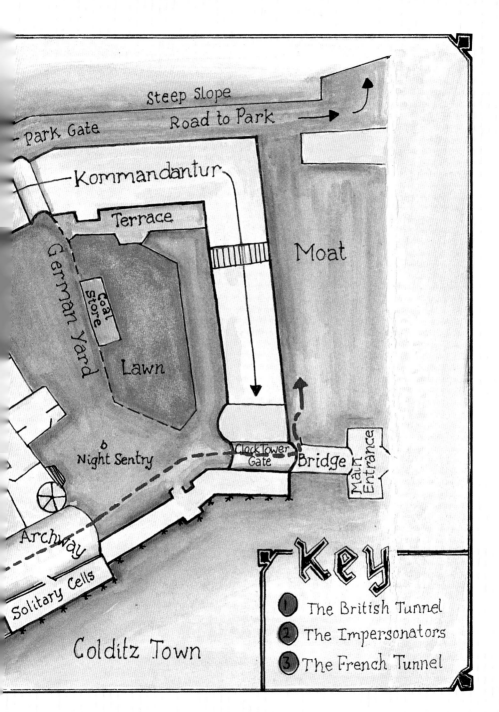

Steep Slope

Park Gate

Road to Park →

Kommandantur

Terrace

German Yard

Coal Store

Lawn

Moat

б Night Sentry

Clock Tower Gate

Bridge

Main Entrance

Archway

Solitary Cells

Coldit z Town

Key

1 The British Tunnel
2 The Impersonators
3 The French Tunnel

The British Tunnel

The British planned to dig their way out of the castle by extending a sewer tunnel that ran under the floors, starting at a manhole cover in the floor of the prisoners' canteen. The tunnel was to come out on a terraced lawn on the east side of the castle.

The sewer tunnel was only 61 centimetres by 91 centimetres around. It was smelly, slimy, and dark. Night after night, the men dropped down into the sewer and chipped away at the stones and mortar.

Finally, they broke through the castle wall and tunnelled their way up and out onto the lawn. But they needed to hide the exit from the Germans until the night of their escape. One resourceful prisoner built a small table top on legs that was strong enough to hold the weight of a passing soldier. Turf was cut out to fit on top of the table, and it was plugged into the exit hole.

From that grass-covered exit in the shadow of the stone walls, the prisoners planned to drop down the steep slope below and escape into the park beyond. But they had one big problem – a soldier patrolled the area.

The men decided to bribe him to "look the other way" on the night of their escape. His reward would be 500 **marks**: 100 marks in advance, and the rest to be dropped out of a window after the escape had taken place.

On the evening of May 29, 1941, thirteen prisoners gathered in the canteen and began to crawl through the smelly tunnel on their hands and knees. At the far end, the first man lifted up the table top and clambered out. He looked up at the floodlit castle wall and froze. On the wall, he saw his crouching shadow. Next to it was the shadow of a German officer standing over him, with a gun. "Hände hoch!" ("Hands up!") the figure yelled.

The German guard who had betrayed the escapers kept his 100-mark advance, and received a promotion and extra leave into the bargain. For his own safety, he was transferred from Colditz.

The Dummies

Once a day, the prisoners were marched out of the prison gates along a path to exercise in the castle park. They were counted as they left the castle, and again on their return. It was from this park, in the chilly autumn of 1941, that two daring Dutchmen made their escape. The Dutch had found a manhole cover in the park. It concealed a water conduit about 1 metre square and 2.5 metres deep – big enough to hide in until they could escape when night came.

But what about the body count when the prisoners returned to the castle, and roll-call that night? Wouldn't the guards be alerted and begin a search when the count was two down? The Dutch hit upon a simple scheme. Central to that scheme were two dummies with plaster heads that could be fixed to makeshift frames.

Above: The exercise park
Left: Spot the dummy!
Right: A Dutch officer holds "Moritz"

As the exercising prisoners were counted out of the castle gate that day, the two escaping prisoners crouched out of sight under long black cloaks worn by two of the taller men. Out in the park, when the guards weren't looking, the manhole cover was whipped off and the escapers hid until nightfall.

Back in the castle, the dummy parts were smuggled out into the courtyard under army **greatcoats**, then quickly assembled for evening roll-call. The prisoners draped long coats around the dummies' shoulders and put officers' hats on their heads. Those holding the dummies then took their places in the centre of the middle row.

The Germans counted heads, and the prisoners held their breath, but the guards didn't notice a thing! The escapers had gained vital time for their long and successful journey to the safety of **neutral** Switzerland.

After that, the two dummies, named Max and Moritz, were used in many more escape attempts before they were "captured" by the Germans.

The Tea Chest

By 1942, the number of
prisoners in Colditz had grown, and the
cluttered prisoners' quarters were becoming
difficult for the guards to search. So the
prisoners were given Red Cross tea chests and
told to pack away all unwanted belongings.
These were to be stored in the attics of the
Kommandantur, the German garrison area of
the castle where the guards and their
families were housed. Parts of the
Kommandantur were also used
as storerooms.

Imagine how surprised a German housewife
must have been when she glanced up on
September 8, 1942, to see an 18-metre length
of blue and white bedsheets dangling from
a storeroom window! She alerted the guards,
but, by that time, there was no sign of the
daring escaper. He had hidden in one
of the tea chests, and was carried off
to the attic, where he got out of his box
and lowered himself from a window on
his home-made rope.

He left a cheeky message for the guards in the empty tea chest: "Die Luft in Colditz gefällt mir nicht mehr! Auf Wiedersehen!" ("The air in Colditz no longer pleases me. Goodbye!") A week later, he was recaptured.

The Impersonators

Colditz Castle had two courtyards backing on to each other. One was the prisoners' courtyard. The other yard was surrounded by German administrative buildings, including the Kommandantur. Above the courtyards, the buildings rose three storeys high, with attics above that.

The archway into the prisoners' courtyard

The only access to the prisoners' yard was through the main gate, across a bridge above a dried-out moat, and then through an arched gateway into the larger "German" courtyard. From there, prisoners went through yet another archway with huge doors and heavy iron bars, and along an approach yard to a guardhouse and the POW entry gate. It was through this guardhouse that two prisoners walked to freedom on the night of January 5, 1942, right under the very noses of the guards.

The prisoners had been taking part in a play in the prison theatre, on the top floor. Earlier, they had cut through the floor under the stage, lowered themselves by rope to a locked room below, and found a passage leading out of the prisoners' courtyard. The only problem was that it exited right outside the guardhouse. The solution? They decided to impersonate German officers and walk straight past the guards.

For the plan to work, the escapers needed fake German uniforms, and so Dutch Home Army greatcoats were altered to look like those worn by German officers. Gold stars for the epaulettes, showing their bogus rank, were carved from wood and painted. The uniforms looked correct in every detail – from a distance.

On the night of their escape, the prisoners shimmied down the rope, crawled through the passage, and strode past the guardhouse with the swaggering, authoritative air of German officers.

A Dutch prisoner wearing
a fake German uniform

The guardhouse, which is now the Colditz Escape Museum

A sentry on duty snapped to attention as the "senior officers" passed. The prisoners must have had their hearts in their mouths!

Walking as normally as possible, and now and then exchanging remarks in German, the escapers passed the archway sentry, crossed the German courtyard, and passed through another security gate, before turning out of a gate and into the dried-out moat. Then, just when it seemed that they would make it safely away, a soldier suddenly appeared out of the night and stared curiously at them. In perfect German, one of the prisoners barked angrily at the soldier, "Why do you not salute your superior officers?" The soldier gave a sharp salute, and the prisoners walked on unhindered towards the outer castle wall. Seventy-two hours later, they were both safe in Switzerland.

The French Tunnel

The prisoners' courtyard at Colditz Castle was a cobbled space about 28 metres by 36 metres, hemmed in on all four sides by towering stone buildings. No sunlight could reach here, and it was cold and damp. It must have been freezing out there as the prisoners lined up for roll-call in winter.

On the north side of the courtyard was the prison chapel. It was beneath the floor of this chapel that the French prisoners built the most amazing escape tunnel of the war. Work began on the tunnel in June, 1941. For eight months they scraped, dug, and hacked their way through timber, earth, and even solid rock foundations. Amazingly enough, the Germans knew what they were up to. They could hear the prisoners digging away in the dead of night, but they couldn't find the cleverly hidden entrance!

The prisoners had discovered an old clock tower in the attics of the castle. Its clock weights and chains had been removed years ago, leaving a narrow shaft that dropped 34 metres to the cellars below. The prisoners climbed down a rope, and started the tunnel in a cellar wall.

Right: *The prisoners' yard in winter (1941–42), painted by William Anderson*

The prisoners dug up underneath the wooden floor of the chapel, then horizontally for a distance of 7 metres. They cut through heavy oak timbers 40 centimetres square, using nothing more than table knives. At the end of the chapel, they had to tunnel 5 metres down to get under the castle's stone foundations. From there, they dug along a further 14 metres with two more descents, reaching beyond the castle wall. Rubble from the tunnel face was moved out in sacks on sleds, and then hauled up the clock tower by rope pulley and dumped in the castle's attics.

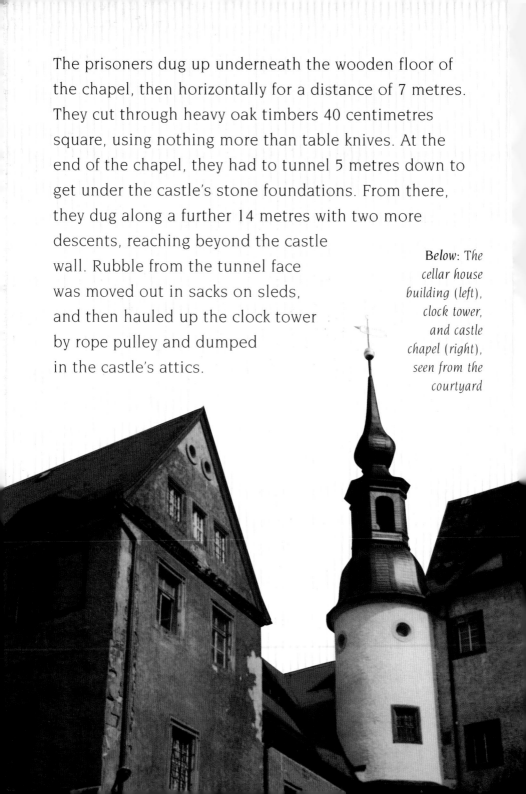

Below: The cellar house building (left), clock tower, and castle chapel (right), seen from the courtyard

The tunnel was a great feat of engineering. It even had electric lighting! The prisoners had wired their circuits into the chapel's electricity supply. Light bulbs lit the way for the tunnellers, and were also used as a warning signal if guards were nearby.

Above: A ladder leading down into the French escape tunnel under the castle chapel

Tunnelling went on into 1942. The Germans were driven mad by the cockiness of the French, who knew that the noise of their tunnelling could be heard. The guards searched every part of the castle, but couldn't find a thing. Then, on January 15, the Germans heard noises in the clock tower. They lowered a boy down the shaft, and the tunnel was found. The French had needed only another 15 metres of digging to complete the tunnel. Instead, the two ringleaders were punished with solitary confinement, and money from the prisoners' canteen profits was confiscated to pay for repairs to the sagging, debris-damaged attic roofs.

Above: *Tins of German, British, and French food were discovered in the tunnel.*
Left: *William Anderson painted this picture in 1942, during one of several spells in solitary confinement.*

The Colditz Glider

The chapel was also the staging point for another fantastic escape plan. British prisoners came up with the idea of making a glider in which two men could be catapulted from the castle roof. In May, 1944, detailed plans were drawn up, and work began behind a false plaster wall in an empty attic above the chapel.

They made the nose cone of the glider out of papier mâché. Floorboards were used for the rest of the framework, which was covered in blue and white checked bedsheets. Bedsheets also covered the 5-metre wings. On the day of the flight, the prisoners planned to smash a hole in the attic wall and carry the glider parts out onto the roof. The glider would then be assembled on a trolley joined by pulleys to a bathtub filled with concrete. The prisoners calculated that, when the bathtub was dropped 18 metres through the floor, it would provide enough thrust to propel the glider over the castle walls!

The prisoners had completed the glider in January, 1945, when word came through of the Allied advance across Europe. The end of the war was in sight. The escape attempt was called off and, on April 15, 1945, American troops stormed into Colditz and freed the prisoners.

The prisoners had good reason to celebrate. Colditz Castle hadn't beaten them. More than 300 escape attempts were made from Colditz, and 130 prisoners actually succeeded in getting away from the castle, but were later recaptured. Another 30 successfully reached home – the best escape record of any prisoner of war camp in Germany.

Above: The original Colditz glider
Right: The glider was destroyed after the war. Recently, however, a documentary team reconstructed it, based on the prisoners' plans. Here, former Colditz prisoners Bill Goldfinch, 83, who drew up the original plans, and Jack Best, 87, who helped to build the original glider, celebrate the successful launching in Hampshire, England, February 2000. "That was beautiful," said Bill Goldfinch. "I always thought it would fly."

Glossary

Allies (*adj*: **Allied**) – Great Britain and the countries that were allied with it during both world wars, including, *in World War* I (1914–18): Russia, France, Belgium, Italy, Japan, and, after 1917, the USA – eventually, more than twenty countries; *in World War* II (1939–45): France and the Commonwealth countries; also, after 1941, the USA, China, and the USSR. By the end of the war, fifty countries had joined the Allies

Commonwealth – an association of countries that were previously part of the British Empire

concentration camp – a camp for the detention of political prisoners

flak – anti-aircraft fire

greatcoat – a long, heavy overcoat, usually military

mark – the basic unit of German money

Morse code – a signalling system in which letters are represented by long and short electronic sounds or flashes of light

neutral – a country not allied with either side during a war

prisoner of war (POW) – a person who is captured and imprisoned during war

Resistance – an underground movement formed in France during World War II to fight the German occupying forces. Also, the Belgian Resistance, formed in German-occupied Belgium, World War I.

From the Author

This book was inspired by two very different experiences. Some years ago, I travelled through Europe and visited the war graves of soldiers killed in World War I. I'll never forget the haunting sight of all those crosses stretching out across the fields. Neatly mown lawns surround the crosses now, but, in my mind's eye, I could see the fields as they would have been in battle: muddy and cratered and littered with bodies. I couldn't get John McCrae's beautiful poem "In Flanders Fields" out of my head.

As a child, one of my favourite television programmes was a series called *Colditz*. It was about prisoners of war in Germany during World War II. The prisoners were always planning daring escapes and outwitting their German guards. But it wasn't until I was older that I learned that Colditz actually did exist, and that many brave men risked their lives trying to escape from its walls.

I hope you enjoy reading the stories of some of these brave people as much as I enjoyed learning about them.

Susan Brocker

If you have enjoyed reading *War Heroes*,
read these other chapter books.

A Rose on the River
Glory Gate
Across the Oregon Trail
The Riddle of the Seaplanes
The Genie of the Bike Lamp
Fibonacci's Cows
The *Mary Celeste* Mystery